OUR HEART

For all believers everywhere, we present an opportunity to receive power from God. We offer ourselves as evidence that God uses the unqualified when we're willing to take a risk. We strengthen each other through community & theology, and we call out to all those who feel ill-equipped, isolated, and hungry, saying: you belong. To the sick, we offer a community of faith that will believe for your healing. To the skeptic, we offer our stories and our lives as fruit of Jesus' work. Come receive from God what you need; come learn how to take risks in your faith; come join us as we each fulfill God's dream for us.

We are a global community of believers empowered to awaken the world.

Walking in the Wilderness

Walking in the Wilderness by William Wood

© Copyright 2017 William Wood

All rights reserved.

ISBN: 978-1-944238-17-9

Edited by: Amanda Bergette Vigneaud, Susan Thompson, and Bob Baynard

No part of this book may be reproduced, stored or transmitted in any form or by any means, electronic or mechanical, including photocopying and recording, or by any information storage or retrieval system, except as may be expressly permitted in writing by the publisher. Requests for permission should be addressed in writing to:

Apostolic Network of Global Awakening 1451 Clark Street, Mechanicsburg, PA 17055

For more information on how to order this book or any of the other materials published by Global Awakening, please contact the Global Awakening Bookstore.

All Scripture quotations, unless otherwise indicated, are taken from the Holy Bible, New International Version®, NIV®. Copyright ©1973, 1978, 1984, 2011 by Biblica, Inc.™ Used by permission of Zondervan. All rights reserved worldwide. www.zondervan.com The "NIV" and "New International Version" are trademarks registered in the United States Patent and Trademark Office by Biblica, Inc.™

Cover typography and layout by Daniel St. Armand.

Photograpphy by Derek Thompson

Walking in the Wilderness

WILLIAM WOOD

globalawakening
lighting fires • building bridges • casting vision

Contents

Introduction

Chapter 1
Yielding to the Spirit

Chapter 2
Governed by the Father

Chapter 3
Asserting Your Authority

Chapter 4
Embracing the Process

Chapter 5
Encountering Living Waters

Conclusion

INTRODUCTION

But Jesus Himself would often slip away to the wilderness and pray.
Luke 5:16

For too long, the church has adopted a mindset that has warred against God's intentions for the wilderness. Because our perspective often determines the level of promises we can receive, this perspective has held us back from receiving the promises God wants to fulfill in and through us during this season. I am confident that God wants to shift the church's perspective on the wilderness season to reclaim this territory in our lives and to position us for unimaginable breakthrough. Far from being a desolate wasteland, I believe the wilderness exists for you and me to discover Christ as our river source.

What do you imagine when you hear the word wilderness? Is it a good or bad place? Is it empty or fruitful? Most of us would contend that a wilderness season is generally understood as a journey through a dry and barren land. However, Luke 5:16 tells us that Jesus Himself would often slip away to the wilderness and pray. If Jesus retreated to the wilderness, what can we learn from Him and His journey there?

In my lifetime, I have sojourned through many wilderness seasons. In these journeys, the Lord has taught me how to "see the goodness of the Lord in the land of the living," even in the midst of testing, trial and tribulation (Psalm 27:13). As I have learned to allow God to lead me through my own walks in the wilderness, I have begun to view the territory there in a completely different light. By looking to Christ as my example, I now see the wilderness for what it was always intended to be: a place for refreshment and renewal where we can commune freely with the Father.

All around the world, God is raising up a generation of believers who are learning to walk well in the wilderness. This generation of believers is taught directly by the Triune God and is in the process of fully maturing in Christ, meaning that Satan has no influence in their hearts. Even through the desert land, these mature sons and daughters follow Christ's footsteps and walk like Him: they are yielded to the Spirit and governed by the Father's voice. Filled with the Word, they have walked through the wilderness as passionate worshippers and have emerged as victorious warriors.

Until we can view the wilderness from God's eyes, we will miss the benefits of walking through it. If we truly want to learn how to handle the wilderness season, receiving the fullness of God's purposes for us in the journey, we must turn to the first and only mature Son of God as our example. As you read this book, I hope that you will allow God to renew your understanding of the wilderness. As you do, I believe that the very place you have perceived as a dry and barren land will become an oasis for you to discover rivers of His Living Water.

CHAPTER 1
YIELDING TO THE SPIRIT

Then Jesus was led by the Spirit into the wilderness to be tempted by the devil. Matthew 4:1

Many years ago the Lord gave me a dream. Since then, I've been pondering the dream in my heart and meditating on its meaning. In this dream, I was standing before a great forest and I knew it represented a wilderness. Suddenly, men and women emerged out of the forest and over each of their heads I saw the words, "Matures Son, Mature Daughter." When I emerged from the dream, I immediately understood that God is raising up a generation of mature believers - sons and daughters who are firmly established in their identity. This excites me! As I've matured in my faith, the Lord has grown this vision inside of me and I have been deeply transformed. In many ways, the dream was the birth of a new life message in my heart, as well as the beginning of this message.

There has only been one mature son to ever walk the earth - our Lord, Jesus Christ. The good news is that we are made in His image. In the same way that Jesus is a son of heaven, we are created to be like Him in our relationship with the Father. As He exists in unity with the Father, so are we called to be like Him through intimacy. As Jesus operates in ministry, so are we created to be like Him in the world. In the same way Jesus moves in sonship, we are called to be like Him in power and authority. In the same way Jesus grew in wisdom and in stature throughout His life, we are created to be like Him as we grow in maturity.

> *So Christ himself gave the apostles, the prophets, the evangelists, the pastors and teachers to equip the saints for the work of ministry for the building up the body of Christ, until we all attain to the unity of the faith and of the knowledge of the Son of God, to mature manhood, to the measure of the stature of the fullness of Christ, so that we may no longer be children, tossed to and fro by the waves and carried about by every wind of docvtrine, by human cunning, by craftiness in deceitful schemes.*
>
> *Ephesians 4:12-13*

Ephesians 4 explains that the purpose of ministry is to equip the saints so that all main attain unity, knowledge of God, and maturity in Him. I believe this is particularly true as we learn to walk in seasons of wilderness. I am convinced that if we can yield to the Spirit and obey the voice of the Father in a seemingly dry and weary land, we will begin to mature like Christ. As we allow God to grow us to the measure of the stature of the fullness of Christ, we will stand firm and steadfast amidst the waves and winds of the devil's crafty schemes no matter where we are.

Matthew 4 says, "Then Jesus was led by the Spirit into the wilderness to be tempted by the devil." Who led Jesus into the wilderness? The Spirit of God! It compelled Him to go. As Christians, it can be easy for us to view times of trials and tribulation as seasons deriving from the camp of the enemy. When we do this, we may avoid or try to escape the wilderness season before God has fully accomplished His purposes in us. Whenever we face testing of any kind, we must look to Jesus as our model. When we look at the blueprint of His life, we cannot overlook this detail of His journey.

Immediately after baptism, Christ allowed Himself to be led into the wilderness by the Spirit.

> At that time Jesus came from Nazareth in Galilee and was baptized by John in the Jordan. As Jesus was coming up out of the water, he saw heaven being torn open and the Spirit descending on him like a dove. And a voice came from heaven: 'You are my Son, whom I love; with you I am well pleased.' At once the Spirit sent him out into the wilderness, and he was in the wilderness forty days, being tempted by Satan.
>
> Mark 1:9-12

Why did the Spirit of God send Jesus into the wilderness directly following baptism? Because it was in baptism that Jesus received both a powerful affirmation and acceptance from the Father. Named and embraced as a son, Jesus was armed with the truth of sonship and wooed into complete surrender to the Holy Spirit. Filled with the Spirit and equipped with the impenetrable armor of the truth of His identity, Jesus was fully prepared to stand His ground against any lie the enemy would try to use against Him.

If the Spirit of God led Jesus into the wilderness, what does this teach us about God's purposes? We serve a good God and can trust that He works all things together for our good. If the Spirit of God led Jesus into the wilderness, you better believe it was for Jesus' benefit! Why did He do this? Was He leading Jesus into a curse? No! The Spirit will only ever lead us into promise. So what was God doing? God knew Jesus had fully yielded to the Spirit, and therefore was fully equipped to withstand the enemy's temptation. Did the Spirit lead Jesus to the wilderness without a plan? Of course not! God was setting Jesus up for breakthrough and victory. The Spirit's purpose was not only for Jesus to confront the devil; it was for Jesus to conquer him. Before Jesus' public ministry began, it was critical that Jesus defeat Satan in private before he triumphed over him in public. Why is this? Because no one can have a public display of authority of something that's defeating them in private. The Spirit led Jesus to confront the enemy when no one was watching to prove that Satan had neither a hold over Jesus' heart nor the work of His hands.

> *And if the Spirit of him who raised Jesus from the dead is living in you, he who raised Christ from the dead will also give life to your mortal bodies because of his Spirit who lives in you.*
>
> Romans 8:11

What does the example of Jesus mean for your walk in the wilderness? Romans 8:11 says, "the Spirit of him who raised Jesus from the dead is living in you." In the same way that the Spirit led Jesus on a walk through the wilderness, He wants to draw you into a training ground so you can learn to be fully yielded to Him in order to overcome the temptations of the enemy. Most moments of temptation come in private, seemingly insignificant moments when others are not watching. It's in these moments that we have to identify which spirit we want to give our yes. If we allow Satan to influence an insignificant moment, we will empower him to influence our heart. However, if we yield to the Holy Spirit in a moment of temptation, we will exercise our authority over the enemy and our integrity will be refined.

When I was in ministry school, I lived in a community house with about 30 other believers. We shared a pantry, and each member of the house had a designated area where they stored their food. One thing to know about me is that I adore peanut butter and honey sandwiches and I eat one every day. One day, I was out of honey, but I noticed that my neighbor had a perfectly unopened bottle of honey on one shelf above mine. Suddenly, I found myself in a battle contemplating whether or not to steal! I only needed a small amount of my neighbor's honey and I knew I could take some without them ever knowing. But I had to remember, what seems to be very insignificant in the natural will carry a great measure of significance in the spiritual. I knew I couldn't take the honey, as seemingly insignificant as the act seemed. Though that moment wasn't necessarily the wilderness, it was a moment of temptation that forced me to identify which spirit I wanted to submit my will to. If I had allowed the voice of the enemy to tempt me into sin, even in that trite moment, I would have surrendered part of my heart to him. But because I said no to his voice, I was able to conquer the enemy from a place of influence and authority.

I believe the wilderness season is actually one of the most profound seasons of life we can experience because it's the place where the Spirit defines and matures our character and integrity. God calls and equips us to confront Satan in private so that we can demonstrate our authority over him in public. What's amazing is that our ability to overcome is not measured by anything other than our yes, our yielding to the Spirit. When you yield, you recommit your will to God and surrender your heart to Him. In doing so, you permit God to flow in and through you so you are empowered to live like Jesus.

I remember when the Lord really began to teach me about yielding completely to the Holy Spirit. About one year after my salvation, my friend and I were doing street ministry five to six times a week. We would typically minister about six or seven hours at a time by blessing and praying for people. One day we had finished ministering and were driving home when I saw a crow fly by my window. As I saw this crow fly in the opposite direction from where we were going, I heard in my spirit the words "direction to death." I didn't know what to do with those words, so I shared them with my best friend, Woody, who was driving the car. I told him, "Woody, I just saw this bird fly by the car window and in my spirit I heard the phrase "direction to death." Before I could fully finish my sentence, my friend Woody had turned the car around to follow the bird's path. Now, I know this sounds a little crazy, but how would we have known if it was the Holy Spirit if we didn't risk a little?

As we turned around, we are stunned to realize that the bird was actually flying directly over the middle of the road making it easy for us to follow him. I couldn't believe it! Sure enough, after just a few minutes, the bird turned down a driveway, flew over a home and landed in a tree! As I was wondering what we should do next, Woody barreled down the driveway after the bird and pulled our car up to the front door of the house. As we approached the home, we saw a man standing on the front porch with a gun in his hand. My first thought was, "Oh God, what if the devil was speaking to us and this is a direction to our death?" But before I could process my thoughts, Woody rolled down the window and the following words fell out of my mouth: "Excuse me, sir. We feel the Lord led us here because someone in your house is dealing with death." Immediately, the man dropped his gun on the ground and began to weep. He responded, "My son is in the hospital, dying from pneumonia. The doctors don't think he's going to live until tomorrow." In that moment, I began to recognize what God can do through us when we yield even when it makes no sense in the natural. When we told this man that God had sent us to him to pray for his son, the power of God suddenly invaded this man's life. I am still amazed that because we said yes to the Holy Spirit, a moment was created for an entire family to encounter the power and presence of God.

As we prepared to leave the house, we saw the crow depart from the tree. Woody and I looked at each other and decided we didn't want to stop following him! As the crow flew out over the highway, we followed behind him. As silly as it sounds, we were just so passionate about what God could do through us that we had to see where the crow would go next! We followed him down a dirt road and, sure enough, the bird flew over another home and landed in a tree! We pulled into the driveway and found a woman sitting on her front porch weeping. We stepped out of the car and said, "Excuse me, ma'am. We feel that God led us here to pray for you. Are you dealing with anything that needs prayer?" The woman looked up at us and responded, "I just lost my husband and son in a car accident six months ago and I don't believe God is real or that He loves me anymore."

Woody and I decided to sit with this woman for about an hour and a half and just cry with her. All of a sudden, the power of God began to touch all three of us. By the end of our time together, we had shared the story of following the crow to her house. Her response to that was, "God has to be real to send two crazies to follow a bird to my house just to tell me He loves me." God will do anything to show His love to the lost!

I grew so much from the "following the crow" experience. Your level of trust to follow Him determines the level of your obedience. How often do we feel the Spirit move us, but we don't trust the movement enough to obey? The ironic end to this story was the woman's words to us after we finished sitting with her for a few hours. As we're preparing to go home, she told us that her next-door neighbor was a pastor who was dying of an incurable disease. Remembering the words direction to death, we went to the pastor's house, knocked on the door and told his wife, "Good afternoon, we're here to pray for your husband. We feel like God wants to heal him." The woman looked me straight in the eyes while stating, "We do not believe in healing," before shutting the door in my face.

It is a sad reality when the world expresses a greater measure of openness to God than the church does. I believe there is an emergent generation of believers coming forth out of the wilderness season who have learned to surrender their hearts and wills to God. This sold-out generation has turned their whole hearts over to God, giving a complete yes to pursue whatever the Father is doing.

In modeling a life of complete surrender, Jesus showed us what the wilderness season represents: a place of yielding to the Spirit. Because the Holy Spirit loved Jesus and wanted to lead Him into His destiny, we must conclude that God always intended the wilderness to be a place of overcoming. Even though Jesus was tempted by the devil, yielding to the Spirit had already equipped Him for victory. In the same way, I see that this emergent, sold-out generation is learning what Jesus knew when He confronted Satan: that God's strategy is to defeat the devil through mature sons and daughters yielding to His Spirit.

CHAPTER 2
GOVERNED BY THE FATHER

After fasting forty days and forty nights, he was hungry. The tempter came to him and said, "If you are the Son of God, tell these stones to become bread." Matthew 4:2-3

What's interesting about the story of Jesus in the wilderness is that Satan attacks Jesus when He is weakest in His flesh. How many of us know that the enemy will always wait for an opportune time to attack us? He looks at Jesus in the natural, in the flesh, and views it as the perfect time for attack. What is the first thing that Satan attacks? Jesus' identity! Satan says, "If you are the Son of God." Why does he use these words in particular? It's because if Satan could have caused Jesus to doubt who He was, he could have caused Jesus to abort His assignment. That's why he comes to Jesus and says, "if you are the Son of God."

Jesus was able to withstand the enemy's attack because He had just heard the voice of the Father affirming both His sonship and His pleasure in Jesus as a son. How many of you know in your mind that you are a son, but still need to hear the voice of the Father singing His pleasure over you? Some of us are accustomed to hearing God speak, but have not fully given ourselves over to Him to allow Him to lavishly love us the way He wants. Others among us may struggle to hear from God and, for those, it may appear that God is silent. I would like to suggest that, if you are in a relationship with God and are experiencing a season of silence, God is actually inviting you to know and hear Him in a deeper way. I believe the appearance of silence is actually a sign that it's time for you to grow, to step to the next place in your relationship with God. He is not silent. God is always speaking, but He may be speaking outside of the box in which you're accustomed to hearing Him.

So many of us understand our sonship theoretically, but desperately need to experience the Father speaking over us the words, "You are my son, my daughter, in whom I am well pleased." The enemy knows that destiny flows out of identity, which is why he tries so hard to undermine our ability to hear the Father's voice singing over us. When we allow Satan to attach himself to our identity, we permit him to shape our destiny. The enemy has tried to pervert so many destinies by planting lies in the minds of the children of God.

How do you know if your mindset is being sabotaged by the enemy? By examining your beliefs and determining which, if any, undermine what God says about you. You see, truth will always call you to a higher place because truth reinforces purpose. Sometimes, it's easier for us to believe lies because lies don't require anything from us. Truth, on the other hand, calls us to a different, Kingdom-centered reality. It requires effort and agreement with heaven, which pulls us into our created purpose and calling. Living in a lie is like chaining ourselves inside of a prison cell; when truth approaches us, it opens the door to freedom. Jesus is the Truth who opens the door to our freedom, but He will never force us to walk through it. He brings liberty to the captive, but it is our responsibility to embrace it when He arrives at the door of our distorted thinking.

Some of us would prefer to remain locked in our prison cells rather than walk into the light of liberty. Sometimes walking through the door feels like too much of an effort. The problem is, the longer you believe a lie, the more it defines you. The deeper the lie embeds itself in our minds, the harder it becomes to uproot. For some of us, our entire identities are built around the lies inside of us rather than the truth spoken by the Father over us. That's when we become the most vulnerable to the attacks of the enemy. With our hearts and minds at risk, we stumble through the wilderness instead of stomping on the enemy's head. I refuse to give Satan the right to conform my identity because I know who I am!

I believe that every person's heart is longing to know the truth of their identity and to hear the Father's voice speaking His pleasure over them. Some of us have been walking manifestations of childhood lies for our entire lives. Instead of receiving the title of son or daughter, we have accepted the enemy's label of unloved, abandoned, worthless and purposeless. Instead of being conformed into the image of the Truth, we live up to nothing more than the lies we hear in our head.

> *Jesus said, "If you hold to my teaching, you are really my disciples. Then you will know the truth, and the truth will set you free."*
>
> John 8:31-32

The good news is that the Father is the source of truth, and His truth will set us free from the bondage of deception. All we have to do to be governed by the Father is to embrace the reality that we are sons and daughters of a good Father. As we make the choice to follow Him and partner with truth, we become divinely equipped to walk into the wilderness and destroy the lies of Satan. We not only survive the wilderness, we flourish there. Many times the difference between life and death in the wilderness season simply boils down to our will - are we willing to partner with God's truth about us? Do we really want to change, or have we become so defined by our lies that we have actually begun to like our distorted life? As always, we must look to Jesus in order to understand how to deal with and engage our own wills to seek unity with the Father.

> *We know that we have come to know him if we keep his commands. Whoever says 'I know him,' but does not do what he commands is a liar, and the truth is not in that person. But if anyone obeys his word, love for God is truly made complete in them. This is how we know we are in him: Whoever claims to live in him must live as Jesus did.*
>
> *1 John 2:3-6*

1 John 2 says that if I abide in Jesus, I must walk as Jesus walked. In other words, one's actions reveal their master. Too often we proclaim God by doctrine, but walk with Satan by principle. Jesus' walk in the desert revealed that He was fully governed by the Father during His entire time there. When the enemy came to question Jesus' identity, Jesus stood firm on the words He had just heard from the Father at His baptism. It's time for the Body of Christ to stand firm in our identities, just as Jesus did in the wilderness! It is time for the Body of Christ to discover that we are sons and daughters of the most high King, and that the wilderness season is designed to solidify our identity in Christ. Scripture says that power is made manifest in our weakness. When Satan came to Jesus and tested His identity, what appeared in the flesh to be a very weak vessel was actually a yielded, (and therefore powerful) force that could not be overthrown. The wilderness season isn't about exposing your weakness; it's about revealing how Christ has become your strength!

It is possible to be so hidden in Christ that Satan can't even see you. It is possible to be so submitted to and governed by the Father that when the devil looks at you, he only sees Jesus. Our ability to be governed by God is determined by the degree to which we abide in Him. Jesus modeled the life and lifestyle of a believer.

The wilderness season is designed for us to discover our own unique significance in Christ, our originality. Everybody is born an original, but most people die a copy. Most people only want to be someone else because they haven't discovered the purpose of their own unique identity. Comparison is the sacrifice of contentment: when you compare yourself to someone else you are no longer content with who God created you to be. The truth is that you are a unique creation and no one can release an expression of God the way you can. The body is incomplete without you. When you fail to realize your unique significance in Christ, you rob the world of a complete representation of Jesus and you become vulnerable to the enemy's attacks.

When Satan attacked Jesus, he found one who understood His identity. He found one who was so secure and rooted in sonship, He could not fall victim to the lies of the enemy. A complete representation of Jesus to the world begins with sons and daughters who know who they are in Christ. The wilderness season exists for you to discover the significance of your originality so that you can understand you have a creative expression that no one else in the world can release. When you understand who you are, you cannot be deceived by a lie or misguided from your destiny.

In what other ways did Satan attack Jesus? He said, "If you are the Son of God, command that these stones become bread." Jesus' responded, "It is written, Man shall not live on bread alone, but on every word that comes from the mouth of God." Satan asked this question not only to attack Jesus' identity, but also to use Jesus for his own purposes. Satan tried to attach himself to Jesus' identity to command something to happen. When we allow Satan to become the one that defines our identity, he will actually become the one who influences our authority. If Satan could have influenced Jesus' authority, he would have done so with the purposes of bringing about his own works on the earth. I refuse to live my life in a way that authorizes the works of Satan. That's why the wilderness season is so crucial: it forces us to listen to the voice of the Father.

> *Therefore, if anyone is in Christ, he is a new creation. The old has passed away; behold, the new has come.*
>
> 2 Corinthians 5:17

Jesus overcame the second attack of the enemy because He was fully governed by the Father's voice. When He declared that man shall live on "every word that comes from the mouth of God," He reinforced His submission to the Father. Because He had already yielded to the Father in the secret place, He had no problem combatting the lies of the enemy. Jesus yielded, not as God, but as a man in order to demonstrate to all of humanity what is possible when we surrender to the Spirit. This reality is fully available to us today because of what Scripture says: old things have passed away and we are a new creation in Christ. For those who are born again of the spirit, you have the nature of Christ. Through Him, we are empowered and emboldened in our new nature to be fully governed by the Father's voice.

The voice we yield to in private is the one towards which we develop sensitivity. When Satan comes to us and tempts us in seemingly insignificant moments or private situations, we must learn to ignore his voice and refuse his influence over our lives. If we don't, we actually desensitize our ability to hear the voice of the Father. When this becomes a pattern, we will confuse the voice of Satan with the voice of the Father. Over time, we will live our life in such a way that we proclaim God by doctrine, but promote Satan by principle.

Your actions will always reveal the master you serve. I can tell you I love Jesus and that I'm a follower of Christ, but if my actions don't reveal those things then who am I really serving? Too many times, Christians either serve God in our own name or we serve ourselves in God's name. Either path is sin. It's easy to get into a situation where we are conformed Christians, but not transformed believers. That's why the wilderness season exists: to teach us in private, when no one else is watching, how to hear the voice of our heavenly Father. Until we see the wilderness as a privileged period of time to fall before the Father in private, declaring with our words and our actions whose voice has preeminence in our lives, we will never value the wilderness season.

CHAPTER 3
ASSERTING YOUR AUTHORITY

Then the devil took him to the holy city and had him stand on the highest point of the temple. "If you are the Son of God," he said, "throw yourself down. For it is written, 'He will command his angels concerning you, and they will lift you up in their hands, so that you will not strike your foot against a stone.' Jesus answered him, "It is also written, 'Do not put the Lord your God to the test.'" Matthew 4:5-7

Now the serpent was more crafty than any other beast of the field that the Lord God had made. He said to the woman, "Did God actually say, 'You shall not eat of any tree in the garden'" And the woman said to the serpent, 'We may eat of the fruit of the trees in the garden, but God said 'You shall not eat of the fruit of the tree that is in the midst of the garden, neither shall you touch it, lest you die.'" But the serpent said to the woman, "You will not surely die. For God knows that when you eat of it your eyes will be opened, and you will be like God..." Genesis 3: 1-4

The enemy is crafty, but he is not creative. He is a manipulator and since the beginning has twisted God's words to deceive the people of God. The tactics of the enemy in Matthew 4 are the same ones the serpent used in Genesis 3 on Eve. So we shouldn't be surprised when we read in Matthew 4:5-7 that the enemy actually came and tried to attack Jesus with the written

Word. But knowing His position and identity as a Son, Jesus couldn't be deceived. What did Jesus know about Himself and the Spirit and His Father that prevented Him from being misled? What can we learn from His encounter with the devil in the desert?

My first takeaway from Jesus' encounter with Satan is that the validity of truth is determined by the spirit who brings it. When Satan used the Word against Jesus, he did so in a way that invalidated its truth. Satan loves to come to us in the appearance of truth, but when Scripture is used to attack believers its nature is deceptive. In the Garden of Eden, what does the serpent say to Eve? "If you partake from the tree you will not certainly die," even though God had already stated "you must not eat from the tree…or you will die." (Genesis 3:3-4) You see, Satan will come to you in a moment where it appears he's telling the truth in order to make God out to be a liar. But God is truth and He cannot lie. When Eve partook of the tree, did she die in the moment? No. But did she die? Yes! Her death was a delayed destruction. Every time you embrace a lie, you empower that lie to distort your present and destroy your future. Agreement with a lie will always undermine your purpose.

> For though we live in the world, we do not wage war as the world does. The weapons we fight with are not the weapons of the world. On the contrary, they have divine power to

demolish strongholds. We demolish arguments and every pretension that sets itself up against the knowledge of God, and we take captive every thought to make it obedient to Christ.

2 Corinthians 2:3-5

So how did Jesus handle Satan's attack? He responded with Scripture, correctly applied, and combatted the enemy's deception with the spirit of truth and wisdom. Every time you embrace a truth, you destroy a lie. The thoughts you entertain determine if your mind becomes a prison or a place of freedom. 2 Corinthians 10 tells us to take every thought captive to the obedience of Christ. Which thoughts are we to take captive? Every thought! That means I'm called to constantly submit my way of thinking to the Word of truth and the mind of Christ.

Satan is only as powerful as you believe him to be. When Jesus went to the cross, He stripped Satan of his authority. The devil still has power, but he doesn't have authority. To whom did Jesus give His authority? To believers! But so many times, we empower the enemy by agreeing with his deception. Satan has already been disarmed. So how do we not rearm a defeated devil? By taking every thought captive.

What holds us back from taking every thought captive and embodying the spirit of truth and wisdom? When we agree with lies over time, strongholds develop in our mind that distort our ability to see God's truths. These strongholds war against the ways of God. The Bible says that we shall know the truth and the truth shall set us free. How many times in life does the truth of God come to us, opening our prison cell doors to freedom, but we still choose to sit in the jail cell of our lies? How many times do we allow these lies to become so entrenched in our identity that we believe they are truth? Every time you believe a lie, you give it power over you. Sometimes we choose to sit in a lie because it appears to be the easier approach; it doesn't require any effort from us. This is heartbreaking, and it's hindering the church's potential. Truth always calls you to a higher place because truth speaks to your created purpose in the Lord Jesus Christ.

When truth opens the door to our prison cell, it is up to us to choose to step into its freedom. It's easy to determine which truth you have empowered because it's evident in your actions. What's important to remember is that truth isn't something that's meant to be remembered and recited. After all, that's how Satan attacked Jesus in the wilderness: with a recitation of Scripture. Instead, truth is meant to be reproduced through you and me. Because truth is personified in Christ Jesus and we are conformed to His image, we are meant to become truth in Him.

I first began learning the significance of this revelation when the Lord spoke to me several years ago. I was praying with a woman who was dealing with cancer. The only truth to which she would anchor herself was that God would never leave her or forsake her. How many of us know that truth brought comfort to her soul, but not a solution to her problem? God wants to move us beyond the truths that just bring us comfort so that we can embrace the truths that bring us into a greater purpose and reality! When you behold Christ as your greatest source of truth, you are pulled into a reality that matures you and transforms you into His image. There is nothing else in the world like it!

> *You must have the same attitude that Christ Jesus had. Though he was God, he did not think of equality with God as something to cling to. Instead, he gave up his divine privileges; he took the humble position of a slave and was born as a human being. When he appeared in human form, he humbled himself in obedience to God and died a criminals' death on a cross. Therefore, God elevated him to the place of highest honor and gave him the name above all other names, that at the name of Jesus every knee should bow, in heaven and on earth and under the earth, and every tongue declare that Jesus Christ is Lord, to the glory of God the Father.*
>
> *Philippians 2: 5-11*

The perspective that I believe God wants to recover in His church is that we can live like Jesus. I believe many of us are afraid or believe the lie that we cannot live like Jesus because He was God. But the reality is that, while on earth, Jesus lived as a human. I believe that when He exerted His power and authority on earth, He did so not as God, but as a son of His heavenly Father. And I believe that same power and authority is fully available to us today. To live like Jesus is a declaration that the same God who lived in Jesus inhabits us. That's what it means to abide in Him while He abides in us, especially through periods of trials and tribulations.

The story of Jesus in the wilderness motivates me to seek Him daily as my source of truth and to hold on to the Word as I walk through periods of testing. It moves me to refuse to give any of the territory of my heart to the lies of the enemy and to go deeper into maturity and transformation in Christ. I have learned that a lie has no power over me unless I agree with it, and I am passionate about equipping the church with this reality. The world is desperate for sons and daughters who are conformed to the image of God's truth! All of creation is waiting for a people to emerge who refuse to give Satan a foothold in their heart; who know that lies have no power unless we come into agreement with them, and who embody truth itself.

Today, there is an emergent generation of believers who have learned to walk with the word of God flowing in them and from them. Feeding on Scripture as their daily sustenance, they not only have the word of God in them. They operate in the spirit of wisdom so they know how and when to apply the Word. When we live this way we assert our authority over the enemy and reproduce the spirit of truth everywhere we walk.

CHAPTER 4
EMBRACING THE PROCESS

Again, the devil took him to a very high mountain and showed him all the kingdoms of the world and their splendor. "All this I will give you," he said, "if you will bow down and worship me." Jesus said to him, "Away from me, Satan! For it is written: 'Worship the Lord your God and serve him only'." Matthew 4:8-10

Therefore God also has highly exalted Him and given Him the name which is above every name, that at the name of Jesus, every knee should bow, of those in heaven, and of those on earth, and of those under the earth, and that every tongue should confess that Jesus Christ is Lord, to the glory of God the Father. Philippians 2: 9-10

In Satan's third and final attack, it's important to note that Satan offered Jesus something that the Father had already promised Him. Jesus is the King of Kings and Philippians 2:10 says that at His name every knee will bow. So what was Satan doing? Satan identified Jesus' destiny, but his goal was to destroy it. When he brought Jesus up to the mountaintop, he offered Jesus a counterfeit inheritance. Furthermore, he was saying if you do as I say, you can receive your inheritance now. Without the spirit of wisdom, it would have been easy to believe that

Jesus had to do something to bring his destiny and inheritance into fruition. The wilderness season exists to teach us how to embrace the patience and process needed to walk out our destiny and receive our inheritance at the right time.

Before I moved to Pennsylvania, I was a pastor in Alabama. I was convinced that I would remain in Alabama and be a pastor for the rest of my life. However, I had a desire to go to the nations and see God move in power. At that time, our church had grown to about 450 members in a small town of only 15,000 inhabitants; our potential to impact the city was incredibly exciting. You can imagine my surprise when the Lord spoke to me and said, "William, I want you to step down from your pastoral position and move to Pennsylvania to serve Randy Clark."

At that time of my life I was single, but my heart's desire was to be married. I was 31 and I had been praying, almost nightly for 10 years, to meet my wife, worshipping even in the most difficult moments. I felt the Lord say, "Go and obey Me, and I will give you the unfulfilled dreams of your heart." I felt in my spirit, this is it. I am about to walk into the next stage of my destiny! It was a huge step of faith for me, because moving to Pennsylvania meant leaving behind everything and everyone that I knew, but I was confident that God was calling me to surrender what I had in order to receive something new He wanted to give me.

I moved to Pennsylvania and started at the Global School of Supernatural Ministry. Before I arrived, I had purposed in my heart that I wasn't going to let anyone know I was a pastor. I knew how to preach, but God had brought me to the school to serve. There was a temptation to expose myself as a preacher and demonstrate my ability, but I held on to the Scripture, "Humble yourself before the presence of the Lord and He will exalt you." (James 4:10) See, it is our responsibility to be humble; it's His responsibility to exalt. Sometimes, we mix up these two actions: we try to exalt ourselves, so He has to humble us. But there is a reason why He calls us to trust Him, and it usually has to do with the outcome of our lives looking differently than what we might expect.

Just before my second year of ministry school began, a young woman from California heard a word from the Lord: "I don't want you to go to Bethel. The place I have for you is at Randy Clark's School of Supernatural Ministry in Pennsylvania." All of a sudden, God moved this young lady across the country and we both ended up in the same community house a few days before classes were scheduled to begin. When I saw her, I knew in my heart that something in my life had instantly changed and that God was repositioning me for a divine purpose.

Not much time passed and the two of us quickly determined that we had a special connection. After a couple of weeks, I felt the Lord say, "She's the promise - the one you've been crying out for 10 years to meet." He reminded me of the many times I had sat in my room, or fallen on my knees, with my eyes to heaven asking if I was called to run the race of life alone or if God would provide a wife for me. Every time He would take me back to those memories, I would remember how He strengthened me with patience and joy and how He matured me to embrace the process He was taking me through.

To make a long story short, from our first conversation in the community house to our wedding day, only four months passed. I had been in a wilderness journey in this area of my life for 10 years, but because I embraced the process with joy and obedience, God met the desires of my heart for partnership in the blink of an eye. On the other side of that wilderness season, I was able to see its value. I learned what it means to be refined by the fire instead of burned by it, and I grew because of it. The process produced a maturity in me that prepared me for my destiny and divine purpose.

I was overjoyed to be married, but there was still a longing in my heart to step into the fullness of my calling in ministry. Again, I chose to worship God and submit to His process. There was a big temptation to make myself known in the context of the ministry school I was attending. I continually submitted to the Lord and refused the voice of the enemy in this area of my life. I reminded myself, "I cannot sacrifice my integrity in order to be noticed by man. I'm here to impress the Father, no one else."

By the end of my second year of ministry school, Dr. Clark asked to have a meeting with me. In that dialogue, he invited me to join him as he traveled and preached. As he spoke, I tried to remain calm and composed on the outside, but on the inside my heart was leaping. I almost did a back flip! After a long season with many trials and great testing, I knew that God was finally bringing me out of the wilderness and into ministry. I knew that God had called me to Pennsylvania for this purpose and that I was stepping into a new stage of my destiny.

It's easy to be tempted to take the easy road - to try to speed up the process or reach for the inheritance we know in our hearts is rightly ours. But God calls us to embrace His timing, to learn to walk through the wilderness season with patience, integrity and joy. In Matthew 4, Satan gives Jesus the option: worship me and I will give you instantaneous inheritance. But Jesus knew that the one He worshipped would ultimately become the master of His life, and He refused to jeopardize His relationship with the Father for instant gratification. In refusing the enemy's enticement, He prioritized the Father's plan and walked out the wilderness fully equipped to embrace His life's purpose.

Romans 12:1 says, "Therefore, I urge you, brothers and sisters, in view of God's mercy, to offer your bodies as a living sacrifice, holy and pleasing to God - this is your true and proper worship." Our worship is to present ourselves as living and holy sacrifices to God. Following Christ requires sacrifice, but when you know your Father, sacrifice is a joyful experience.

The world is looking for examples of how to handle trials and tribulations. I can attest that the wilderness is to teach us how to worship God in patience and joy because I have lived it. If we will walk through the wilderness well, surrendering our hearts wholly in worship, we will emerge as laid-down lovers of God. The more I travel and minister, the more I see that God is raising up a body of believers who demonstrate how to walk well in the seasons of wilderness. Marked by their love for God, these believers worship their way through the wilderness, refusing to bow to deceit or despair. Fully in love with and delighted by their King, they are learning to embrace their identities as sons and daughters, and in doing so present a full representation of Jesus, the ultimate son and lover of God, to the world.

CHAPTER 5
ENCOUNTERING LIVING WATERS

On the last and greatest day of the festival, Jesus stood and said in a loud voice, "If anyone is thirsty, let him come to me and drink. Whoever believes in me, as the Scripture has said, streams of living water will flow from within him." By this he meant the Spirit whom those who believed in him were later to receive. Up to that time the Spirit has not been given since Jesus had not yet been glorified. John 7:37-39

I grew up in drug culture, in a home with alcoholic parents who didn't believe in God. I began drinking at the age of 12 and, by the time I reached 15, I was a full-blown alcoholic and drug addict. I lived in the Bible belt, but I had never heard the Gospel message or one mention of the name of Jesus.

In May of 2005, I overdosed on drugs and was taken to the hopsital. I didn't have a concept of God, but I found myself in a situation from which only an omnipotent, all-loving God could rescue me. The doctors told me I was in renal failure and that my kidneys were almost completely shut down. As the doctors monitored my other organs, they told me that my other major organs were beginning to fail and that they expected me to die at any moment. They told me, "If we cannot get your remaining organs to work, you will die." I was only 20 years old at the time.

As I lay awake in my hospital bed, not knowing if I was going to make it, I began to realize that all of my lifestyle choices had led me to death. I saw my life ending, unsure about what would come next. Lying there that night, I saw a bright light in my room. Let me be clear: I did not see a vision of a light; I saw a real, tangible brightness. Suddenly, a man walked out of the light. He had a brown goatee and was clothed in an all-white linen robe. I watched this man walk to the foot of my bed and sit down on the floor. Suddenly, an actual river of water burst from one of the walls of my room and shot through the wall on the other side of the room. At this point, I had no concept of God, Jesus or the Gospel, but there was a person, a tangible being, standing in front of me with an actual river of water flowing through my hospital room.

The man in white sat down to wash his hands and, as he did, I heard an audible voice speak to me saying, "The waters that you see will purify and cleanse you if you receive Jesus, the Christ, as Lord and Savior." Immediately, the power of God hit me, touched my organs and sent a surge through my entire body. As the power hit me, and I began to experience the One who is named Jesus as the river of life flowed through my hospital room, my heart leapt within me and everything inside of me cried, "Jesus! I want You!" The next morning, when the doctors come in to run tests on my organs, they exclaimed, "Mr. Wood, we cannot explain this, but there is nothing wrong with your kidneys or any of your organs." Jesus had completely healed every inch of my body from the overdose!

Since I was entirely healed, the doctors discharged me from the hospital. In those days, the Lord had been sovereignly restoring my relationship with my earthly father, and so my dad came to the hospital to pick me up. On our drive home, I realized I was speaking in weird languages. My dad, completely confused, asked me, "Boy, what's wrong with you?" I didn't know! But I knew it had something to do with the decision I had just made to follow Jesus.

I knew I needed guidance on my journey with Jesus, so I asked around and found out I needed to read this book called the Bible. As I began to read through it, I understood that I had been speaking in tongues in the car with my dad. I read more and began to notice all throughout Scripture that men and women were having life-changing encounters with God. For months after my first encounter with Jesus in my hospital room, I continued to have mind-blowing encounters with God.

First, I received a letter in the mail saying that my $45,000 hospital bill had been paid in full. After that, even though I had lost my driver's license because of all the DUIs, it was inexplicably reinstated and returned to me in the mail. Then, one of the greatest wonders that occurred during this season took place when I came before a judge for my court hearing. The day I overdosed, the police had found drug paraphernalia in my pockets, so I was required to go to court. When I came before the judge he said, "William, this is very strange, but we seemed to have misplaced the paraphernalia we found on you." I was looking at a third felony along with a potential 10-year prison sentence, but the evidence to condemn me had been sovereignly taken away! The judge said, "There's nothing for me to do, except to charge you a fine for this court appearance in the sum of $666."

My father had chosen to attend the court meeting with me that day. Listening to the judge's word, he stood up in the courthouse and declared, "I will pay the debt in full." Are you catching the symbolism of my story? At every turn of my life, Jesus saved me! He renewed the organs that drugs had destroyed, removed the evidence condemning me, and redeemed the record against me. He saved me from bondage, paid my debts in full and reconnected my spirit to be one with the Father! It was as if Jesus looked at my life and said, "What the enemy has meant for bad in this young man's life, I am going to make good. What the enemy had purposed for hell, I am purposing for heaving. What the enemy tried to destroy, I am going to fully restore."

If you were to ask me, "Why are you so passionate about life?" I would respond by saying it's because I've met someone [Jesus] who thinks I'm to die for. I've met a man [Jesus] who, in spite of everything I've done, hasn't changed His mind about me. As He walked through the wilderness and, ultimately, to the cross, Jesus chose to endure the suffering for the joy set before Him. God is so in love with you and me that not even death can keep Him away. We are His joy!

After I got saved, I found out that some of my friends were Christians, but had never shared the Gospel message with me. That bothers me to my core. How can you encounter Him and not say something to others who don't know Him?

Today, God is calling forth a generation of people who understand what the wilderness season is meant for and who are willing to walk through it with Him. God is calling this generation to be marked by their yielding to the Spirit, dependence on the Father and their love for Word and worship. As they make the choice to be laid-down lovers, these sons and daughters will find rivers of living water and, in the wildness of the desert, they will find the paradise of His presence! Amen!

CONCLUSION

God thinks you are to die for. Do you think He's worth living for? He wants to transform you into the image of His Son to equip you for the wilderness seasons that you will inevitably encounter. He paid the highest price in order to choose you. You have an opportunity to respond to His voice. All you have to do is respond to His love by yielding to His Spirit. In that act of worship, you too will become a part of the emerging generation of God's laid-down lovers.

If you struggle with what it means to yield to God's Spirit, look to Jesus' life. He yielded everything, becoming a humble servant. "Who, being in very nature God, did not consider equality with God something to be grasped, but made himself nothing, taking the very nature of a servant, being made in human likeness. And being found in appearance as a man, he humbled himself and became obedient to death-even death on a cross." (Philippians 2:5-8) Jesus surrendered His reputation for God's reputation. He understood that His reputation was temporary while God's reputation is eternal.

Jesus was born into poverty and obscurity. The circumstances of His conception were suspicious. His teachings and actions were offensive and scandalous to the religious leaders of the day. He had no home, no place to lay His head. He yielded His will to the will of the Father. King Jesus became a servant to all.

When he had finished washing their feet, he put on his clothes and returned to his place. "Do you understand what I have done for you?" he asked them. "You call me 'Teacher' and 'lord,' and rightly so, for that is what I am. Now that I, your Lord and Teacher, have washed your feet, you also should wash one another's feet. I have set you an example that you should do as I have done for you. I tell you the truth, no servant is greater than his master, nor is a messenger greater than the one who sent him. Now that you know these things, you will be blessed if you do them. John 13:12-17

Being a yielded laid-down lover is easier when you know who you are and whose you are. Jesus had no confusion about His identity because He heard the voice of His Father confirming that identity. "Then Jesus came from Galilee to the Jordan to be baptized by John. But John tried to deter him, saying, "I need to be baptized by you, and do you come to me?" Jesus replied, "Let it be so now; it is proper for us to do this to fulfill all righteousness." Then John consented. As soon as Jesus was baptized, he went up out of the water. At that moment heaven was opened, and he saw the Spirit of God descending like a dove and lighting on him. And a voice from heaven said, "This is my Son, who I love; with him I am well pleased." (Matthew 3: 13-17) God publically authenticated the sonship of Jesus, identified Him as the suffering servant spoken of in Isaiah, and spoke words of affirmation over His Son for the mission that lay ahead.

Just as God established Jesus' identity, He has also established our identity through Jesus. "Yet to all who received him, to those who believed in his name, he gave the right to become children of God-children born not of natural descent, nor of human decision or a husband's will, but born of God." (John 1:12-13) Jesus reconciled us to the Father (Romans 5:10) so that we may live fully as beloved sons and daughters of God. How deep is the Father's love for us that He would send His son to die that we might live as His beloved. The devil wants to keep us confused about identity, to keep us thinking that we're sinners, because if we think we're sinners we'll live like sinners. God intends we live in the fullness of our God-given identity, like His beloved Son Jesus, always listening to His Spirit. "The Spirit himself testifies with our spirit that we are God's children. Now if we are children, then we are heirs-heirs of God and co-heirs with Christ, if indeed we share in his sufferings in order that we may also share in his glory." (Romans 8:16-17)

Living in the fullness of our God-given identity means purposefully living from a Kingdom-centered reality, in agreement with heaven in the smallest and largest details of our lives. It means embracing who God says we are rather than living from the lies of the devil. It means stomping on the enemy's head rather than constantly stumbling through one wilderness after another. It means receiving the truth that you are God's beloved, and living conformed to the image of that truth. It means living so hidden in Christ that the devil can't see you. It means being the original God intends you to be and living as a creative expression of Christ who is in you. It means refusing to live your life in a way that gives authority to the works of the devil. Living in the fullness of your God-given identity means listening to the voice of the One who loves you with an everlasting, unshakable love.

When we live secure in our identity we can walk in the authority given to us in Jesus, authority over all things great and small in our lives. When God created us, He gave us authority and dominion over everything on the earth (Genesis 1:26). Sin gave that authority to the devil, but Jesus restored it on the cross and then He transferred it to us.

Then Jesus came to them and said, "All authority in heaven and on earth has been given to me. Therefore go and make disciples of all nations, baptizing them in the name of the Father and of the Son and of the Holy Spirit, and teaching them to obey everything I have commanded you. And surely I am with you always, to the very end of the age."

Matthew 28: 18-20

Jesus is calling us to walk in His complete and unquestionable authority. That means that we have the authority to combat the enemy's deception in the power of the Word of God, with the Spirit of truth and wisdom. Every time you embrace God's truths you destroy Satan's lies. Every time you take every thought captive to Christ, your thoughts are no longer captive to the devil. When we stop agreeing with Satan's lies, we start tearing down the strongholds that hold us captive to his false identity. The more we walk in God's truths, the greater our freedom. God's truths are not just something to be remembered and recited. He intends for His truths are to be reproduced through us as we become more and more conformed to His image as it is personified in Jesus Christ.

Becoming conformed to Christ is a process that takes time and patience. In the wilderness, Satan tried to tempt Jesus to bypass the process set in place by the Father and take His inheritance before the fullness of God's time. (Matthew 4:8-11) "Again, the devil took him to a very high mountain and showed him all the kingdoms of the world and their splendor. "All this I will give you," he said, "if you will bow down and worship me." Jesus said to him, "Away from me, Satan! For it is written: 'Worship the Lord your God, and serve him only.'" (Matthew 4:8-11) Notice what the devil is saying to Jesus in this passage. He is telling Jesus that He [Jesus] can have His rightful inheritance now if He will turn away from God and worship him [the devil]. Satan knew that all the kingdoms of this world are Jesus' rightful inheritance. And he knew that if Jesus were to believe his lie, then He [Jesus] would actually forfeit His inheritance back to him [the devil].

Make no mistake, the devil wants to tempt you to take the easy road, to try and speed up the process to your inheritance, to take his way that leads to destruction. God intends that you embrace His perfect timing and learn to walk through your wilderness seasons with the patience, joy and integrity that is yours in Christ. Like Jesus, you can refuse the enemy's enticements, instead prioritizing God's plan for your life. When you do, like Jesus, you will come out of your wilderness seasons equipped for the purpose God has for your life. Those with hearts surrendered in the wilderness with emerge as laid-down lovers of God.

God has made provision for our wilderness times. He has provided unending streams of living water and placed them within us! "Whoever believes in me, as Scripture has said, rivers of living water will from within them." (John 7:38) The New Living

Translation says, "'Rivers of living water will from his heart.'" God's unending, life-giving provision is within you, residing in your heart! As someone living in communion with Christ, you have the capacity to drink from the river of God, which is the Spirit of God, whenever you are thirsty, and to be a sphere of spiritual influence to the world around you for the Kingdom of God in the power of His Spirit.

In the book of Acts we see the birth of the Church, (Acts 1:1-6:7) and its expansion amidst persecution (Acts 6:8-9:31). In a few hundred years the gospel was taken to every corner of the known world. The early disciples certainly didn't do this in its own power. They did it in the power of God's Spirit that came on them at Pentecost, transforming them and giving them courage to be witnesses for Christ wherever He sent them. Without God's Spirit there would be no church.

Jesus' temptation in the wilderness demonstrates that Satan was defeated by God in the flesh–Jesus Christ. It also shows us that the leading of the Holy Spirit will not always take us into comfortable or easy places. The Holy Spirit forcefully compelled Jesus into the wilderness to confront and defeat the devil. Just as Jesus was tempted and tested, so too will you be tested. And just as Jesus was proven and strengthened for the ministry that was to come, so too will God's Spirit strengthen you for your assignments.

Following God only looks like sacrifice to those who are not fully in love with Him. The world is hungry for examples of how to handle trials and tribulations. If you are a passionate lover of Christ, it doesn't matter what wilderness you walk through or who is standing in front of you. The more you fall in love with Jesus, the more your mind will be renewed to see the wilderness journey for what it was always intended to be. Instead of a dry and weary land, you will see an opportunity to yield to the Spirit, to submit to the Father and to be transformed more into the image of Christ! You will embrace this chance to refuse the lies of the enemy and root yourself in the Word in a way that produces maturity and transformation while catapulting you deeper into your destiny. The world is waiting for you. What are you waiting for?